My dear friends,

Let me give it to you straight...
this is not just another cookbook ...
this is no ordinary chef's guide, and
it certainly isn't a testimonial to
anyone who professes to be a master
of the culinary arts.

Go Go Gourmet is an explosive
transition to Womens Lib, a flat
guarantee that you'll be liberated
from the kitchen-forever-because the
preparation time for every recipe in
this book is not more than thirty
minutes. The actual cooking time
may be longer, but that should
not concern the cook! She (or he)
can be doing just about anything
while the soup is simmering, the
stew is stewing, or the cake is
baking.

This exciting new cooking experience
will work wonders on your family,
amaze your friends, neutralize your
in-laws, transform your enemies
into friends, and utterly captivate
everyone else important to you.

Beverly Ann Ault

Contents

Go Go

Gourmet

Thirty Minutes to Easy Entertaining

Go Go Gourmet

Beverly Ann Ault

Designed and Illustrated by Henry J. Bausili

Published by **Acropolis Books Ltd.**, Washington, D.C. 20009

ACROPOLIS BOOKS LTD.
Colortone Building, 2400 17th St., N.W.
Washington, D.C. 20009

Printed in the United States of America by
COLORTONE PRESS, Creative Graphics Inc.
Washington, D.C. 20009

Designed by Henry J. Bausili

Library of Congress Catalog Number 72-11553
Standard Book Number 87491-341-1

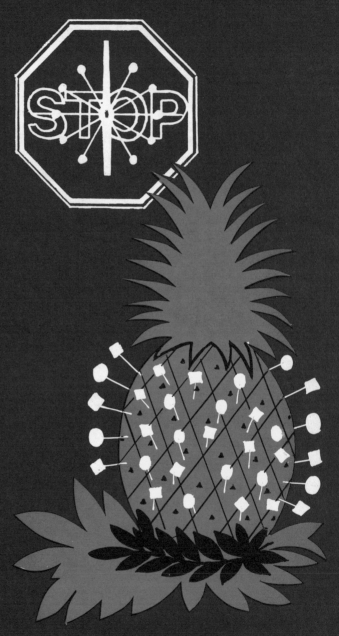

Bits and Pieces

EGGS SIBERIA

The busy woman's answer to deviled eggs.

18 hard boiled eggs, peeled, sliced lengthwise
1 pint sour cream
1 small jar red caviar
Parsley or watercress

Dip teaspoon into sour cream. Fill and invert spoon, putting cream on egg in a smooth mound. When finished, put small dollop of caviar on top of sour cream mound. Surround with parsley or watercress.

Preparation time: 30 minutes

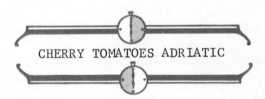

CHERRY TOMATOES ADRIATIC

Colorful and especially delicious when the vegetables are in season.

1 box cherry tomatoes
Olive oil
Lawry's seasoned garlic salt

Toss tomatoes with olive oil; then sprinkle liberally with garlic salt. Pile tomatoes in bowl, place in center of large round platter. Surround tomatoes with pickled okra or marinated green beans (both available at the supermarket), spoke fashion.

Preparation time: 5 minutes

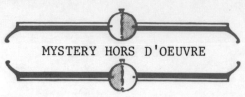

MYSTERY HORS D'OEUVRE

Your guests won't know what they are eating...
keep them guessing!

1 small jar chunky peanut butter
1 jar pitted prunes, cooked
8 strips raw bacon

Stuff each pitted prune with 1 tsp. peanut butter.
Wrap with bacon. Bake at 350 degrees for 20 minutes.

Preparation time: 30 minutes

WINE CHEESE

1 lb. sharp cheddar cheese
1 tsp. Worcestershire sauce
Sherry, about 1/2 cup
Paprika, cayenne, grated nuts, or parsley

Grate cheese. Add Worcestershire sauce and enough
sherry to moisten well. Make into ball or log.
Sprinkle with paprika, cayenne, grated nuts, or
chopped parsley. Keeps well in refrigerator.

Preparation time: 15 minutes

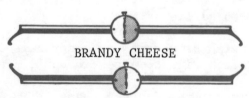

BRANDY CHEESE

1/2 lb. Roquefort cheese
1/2 lb. cream cheese
4 tbs. good cognac or brandy

Put in blender and mix till smooth. Store in crock in
refrigerator. Keeps for months.

Preparation time: 10 minutes

PICKAPEPPA CHEESE

1 small bottle Pickapeppa sauce or A-1 sauce
1 3 oz. package cream cheese
Wheat Thins

Pour Pickapeppa Sauce over cheese. Let stand at room
temperature 15 minutes before serving. Surround cheese
with Wheat Thins.

Preparation time: 5 minutes

CHUTNEY CHEESE

1 bottle chutney
1 8 oz. package cream cheese

Pour chutney over cream cheese and surround with crackers.

Preparation time: 5 minutes

RINGTUM WELCH

1/2 cup chopped frozen or fresh onion
1/2 cup frozen or fresh chopped green pepper
1/4 cup (1/2 stick) margarine
1 lb. sharp cheddar cheese, diced
1 can tomato soup
1 tbs. Worcestershire sauce
1/2 tsp. salt
Dash pepper
1 can Jalepeño relish, drained (optional)

Sauté onion and green pepper in margarine. Add cheese,
stirring constantly; then soup, a little at a time. Add
remaining ingredients. When bubbling hot and smooth,
serve in chafing dish with large tortilla chips.

Preparation time: 15 minutes

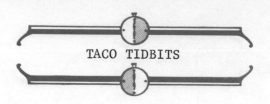

TACO TIDBITS

1 bag Taco chips
8 slices American cheese
1 can Jalapeño relish, drained, or green chilies

Cut cheese to roughly fit Taco chip triangle. Put
1/2 tsp. of relish on top of cheese or thin slice of
green chili. Pop in oven for 10 minutes at 350 degrees.

Preparation time: 10 minutes

IMPERIAL RUSSIAN SECRET

1 small jar red caviar
1 8 oz. package cream cheese
1 small chopped onion

Put chopped onion on cream cheese--then add caviar.
Surround with your favorite cracker.

Preparation time: 5 minutes

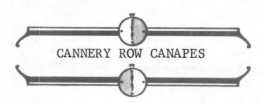

CANNERY ROW CANAPES

8 oz. cottage cheese
3 oz. dry vermouth
1 tbs. white horseradish
1 can minced clams
Juice of 1 lemon

Combine, gradually adding broth from clams until mixture
has the consistency of mayonnaise. Spread on your favorite cracker.

Preparation time: 5 minutes

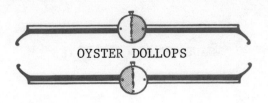

OYSTER DOLLOPS

Super, but simple.

1 can smoked oysters
1/2 pint sour cream
1 box crackers

Put dollop of sour cream in center of cracker and place oyster on top.

Preparation time: 5 minutes

AVOCADO DIP

1 can frozen avocado dip, defrosted
1/2 can chopped green chilies (or more if hotter
    dip is desired)

Add chilies to avocado dip and surround with Taco chips.

Preparation time: 5 minutes

PICKLED SAUSAGE

1 long Italian sausage link, precooked
Sweet pickle juice

Cut sausage into 1/4 inch slices. Soak in pickle juice a minimum of 30 minutes. Sausage keeps nicely in the juice, refrigerated for a week.

Preparation time: 5 minutes

SAUSAGE BISCUIT BITES

1 lb. hot sausage
2 cups grated sharp cheddar cheese
3 cups Bisquick mix

Sausage should be at room temperature. Mix all ingredients with hands. Shape into 1 inch balls. Bake on cookie sheet at 375 degrees, approximately 20 minutes. After first 10 minutes, turn (if you think about it), and continue cooking until done.

This dish freezes beautifully. To reheat, wrap in foil and place in slow oven (300 degrees) for 30 minutes.

Preparation time: 25 minutes

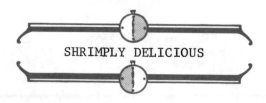

SHRIMPLY DELICIOUS

1 can crab meat
2 cans shrimp, drained
1 tsp. Worcestershire sauce
Juice of 1 lemon
1 cup mayonnaise
1/8 tsp. cayenne
12 Ritz crackers

Pick through crab meat carefully to be sure all shell has been removed. Add shrimp and marinate in lemon juice for 20 minutes. Drain and add Worcestershire sauce and mayonnaise. Then sprinkle in cayenne. Put seafood mixture in Pyrex pie plate. Then crush Ritz crackers with your hand. Sprinkle crackers on top of seafood. Bake 20 minutes at 350 degrees. May be served in small individual clam shells, with seafood forks.

Preparation time: 15 minutes

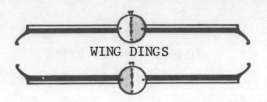

WING DINGS

Flying rave notices!

1 package frozen mini-drums (drummettes) or have
    butcher break apart chicken wing to give
    miniature drumstick (first joint only)
1 large bottle soy sauce

Place mini-drums in shallow pan. Pour soy sauce over
chicken and bake at 200 degrees for 6 hours. Six hours?
Yes, that's right, these are tender and succulent when
cooked for 6 hours, but in a pinch bake at 350 degrees
for 1 1/2 hours.

                              Preparation time: 5 minutes

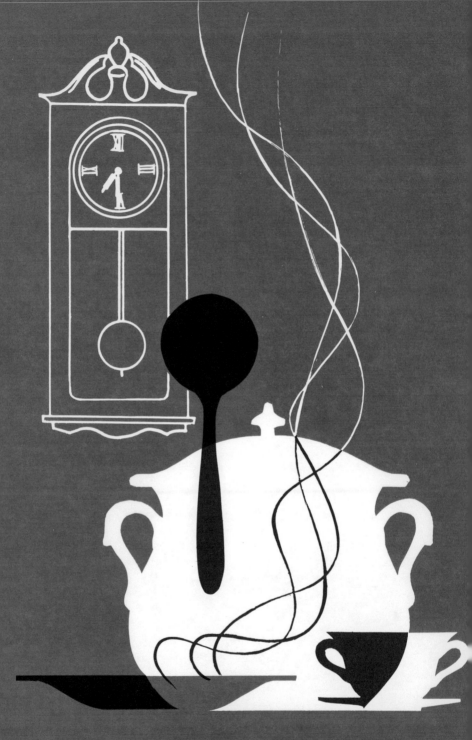

Savory Soups

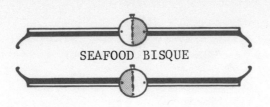

SEAFOOD BISQUE

1 can cream of mushroom soup, undiluted
1 can tomato soup, undiluted
1 can green pea soup, undiluted
1 cup milk
1/2 pint whipping cream
1 can crab meat
1 tbs. Worcestershire sauce
1/2 tsp. Tabasco sauce
Dash celery salt

Combine all ingredients in top of double boiler. Heat over boiling water. Pea soup can be omitted and 1/2 pint light cream and 1 cup sherry added, with no seasonings except salt and pepper.

Serves 6   Preparation time: 15 minutes

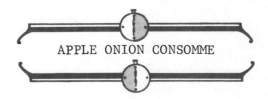

APPLE ONION CONSOMME

1 large apple, cut in chunks
1 large onion, cut in chunks
2 cans beef consommé
1 cup heavy cream
Curry

Peel and boil together apple and onion till tender. Drain and put through very coarse sieve (or Foley food mill). Add consommé. Beat thoroughly. Add heavy cream and beat again. Heat to boiling point. Sprinkle with curry.

Serves 4   Preparation time: 25 minutes

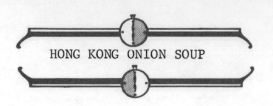

HONG KONG ONION SOUP

2 cans onion soup, diluted
Croutons
1 cup grated sharp cheddar cheese
4 tbs. Parmesan cheese

Prepare soup according to directions on can. Pour
into individual heatproof ramekins. Top with croutons,
Parmesan, then grated cheese. Bake at 375 degrees till
cheese puffs and bubbles, about 20 minutes.

Serves 4-6,   Preparation time: 10 minutes
   depending on size of individual ramekins

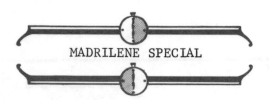

MADRILENE SPECIAL

3 cans red madrilene soup
12 oz. orange juice
2 limes, thinly sliced

Combine the madrilene and orange juice. Stir well.
Chill overnight in refrigerator. Serve ice cold with
lime slice in each bowl or serve piping hot.

Serves 6   Preparation time: 10 minutes

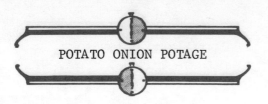

POTATO ONION POTAGE

1 cup chopped frozen or fresh onion
3 tbs. butter or margarine
3 1/2 cups canned chicken broth
1 envelope instant dry mashed potatoes
1 tsp. salt
Dash pepper
1 cup light cream
3 tbs. chopped parsley

Sauté onions in butter or margarine till tender. Add chicken broth and simmer 15 minutes. Add potatoes, salt, pepper, and cream. Simmer gently until heated. DO NOT BOIL. Sprinkle with parsley. May be served hot or cold.

Serves 6   Preparation time: 10 minutes

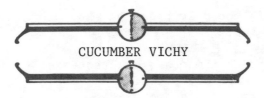

CUCUMBER VICHY

1 can frozen potato soup, defrosted
1 cucumber, peeled and cut into chunks

Buzz cucumber in blender. Add cucumber to soup. Serve chilled. Sprinkle on chopped chives.

Serves 2   Preparation time: 10 minutes

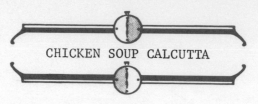

CHICKEN SOUP CALCUTTA

3 cups of chicken soup, diluted
3/4 small container sour cream or
    1 container plain yogurt
1 cup applesauce
Thyme, marjoram, pepper, and curry to taste

Mix all ingredients. Serve ice cold - on ice for
special effect.

Serves 4   Preparation time: 10 minutes

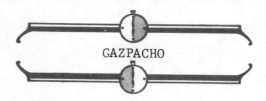

GAZPACHO

This delightful cold soup can be made 3 or 4 days
ahead of serving.

3 canned or fresh tomatoes, well squeezed (reserve juice)
1 cucumber, peeled and sliced
2 green peppers, seeded and sliced
1 small onion, peeled
1 clove garlic
3 tbs. olive oil
3 tbs. wine vinegar
6 slices white bread, trimmed and cubed
3 cups juice from tomatoes, or canned juice
1 1/2 tsp. salt
1/2 tsp. black pepper

Combine all the ingredients in blender and puree until
smooth. Chill very well. Just before serving, check
consistency. The soup should be thick, but drinkable.
Add a little ice water if necessary. Serve in plastic
glasses with 1 cube of ice in each glass.

Serves 6-8   Preparation time: 25 minutes

The Staff of Life

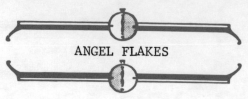

ANGEL FLAKES

Biscuit favorite!

1 package dry yeast
1/2 cup lukewarm water
2 cups buttermilk
1/3 cup sugar
3/4 cup shortening
5 cups self-rising flour (approximately)

Dissolve yeast in warm water. Heat buttermilk until it is lukewarm and dissolves the sugar and shortening. Add yeast to buttermilk mixture, then stir in enough flour to make a soft dough. Turn out on floured surface and knead lightly. Roll to thickness desired, then use juice glass to cut out biscuits. Bake on greased cookie sheets 10 minutes at 425 degrees, or till brown. Dough can be refrigerated for several days before baking. These biscuits freeze nicely after baking and do not crumble when cold.

Yields 150 half-dollar size or 75 dinner size

Preparation time: 15 minutes

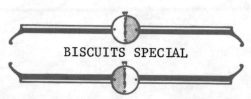

BISCUITS SPECIAL

1 can your favorite refrigerated biscuits
2 tbs. minced instant onions
2 tbs. melted butter

Place biscuits on cookie sheet. Make small hollow in center of each biscuit with bottom of small glass, dipped in flour. Combine onion and butter. Fill hollows with onion mixture. Bake at 450 degrees, 8-10 minutes.

May be made in advance by baking 4 minutes, then refrigerating. When ready to serve, bake 4-6 minutes more in oven at the same temperature.

Serves 6-8   Preparation time: 5 minutes

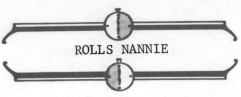

ROLLS NANNIE

Nannie fed the family. Here are some of her quick secrets.

2 1/2 tbs. shortening
2 heaping tbs. sugar
1 package yeast
1 cup warm water
2 cups flour (approximately)
Butter

Dissolve yeast in water. Melt shortening, add sugar.
Add enough flour to thicken like gravy. Mix in dissolved
yeast; add enough flour to make dough quite firm. Let
rise 15 minutes. Pat out with hand and cut into rounds
with rim of small glass. Fold in half and put dot of
butter between fold, if desired. Bake at 400 degrees
for 15 minutes.

Serves 10   Preparation time: 15 minutes

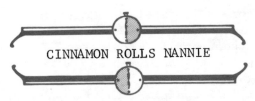

CINNAMON ROLLS NANNIE

Prepare dough according to directions for ROLLS NANNIE.
Let rise 15 minutes. Pat out dough to about 1/2 inch
thickness, spread with softened butter, and sprinkle
with cinnamon sugar. Roll up, jelly roll fashion, and
cut in 1 inch slices. Bake at 400 degrees for 15 minutes.

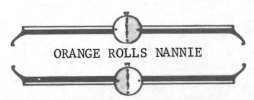

ORANGE ROLLS NANNIE

Follow directions for CINNAMON ROLLS NANNIE, except
spread rolled-out dough with soft butter, then with
orange marmalade thinned with a little orange juice.
Continue following CINNAMON ROLLS NANNIE recipe.

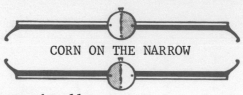

CORN ON THE NARROW

1 small can creamed yellow corn
2 cups Bisquick mix
1/2 cup (1 stick) butter

Mix corn and Bisquick mix. Roll out and cut biscuits.
The thinner they are, the crisper they'll be. Melt
butter and coat each side of biscuit. Bake at 450
degrees about 10 minutes.

Serves 8   Preparation time: 15 minutes

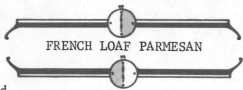

FRENCH LOAF PARMESAN

1 French bread
1/2 cup (one stick) soft butter
1 small container Parmesan cheese
Garlic salt
Paprika

Split French bread lengthwise. Coat each side with
soft butter; sprinkle heavily with Parmesan cheese,
garlic salt, then paprika. Fold two halves back together. Wrap in foil and bake at 350 degrees until
heated through, approximately 20 minutes. Just before
serving, open foil and place halves under broiler until
lightly browned. Remove from oven and cut into slices.

Serves 10   Preparation time: 10 minutes

WINTER ROLLS

Friendly fare on a cold day!

4 large bakery rolls
1 cup sour cream
1/2 can French fried onions, crumbled

Split rolls in half and spread cut sides thickly with
sour cream. Sprinkle with onions. Bake at 325 degrees
for 15 minutes.

Serves 4   Preparation time: 5 minutes

Hearty Fare: Main Dishes

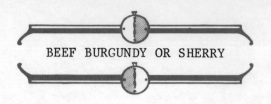

BEEF BURGUNDY OR SHERRY

2 lbs. stew beef
1/2 package onion soup mix
1 small can mushrooms, drained
2 cans golden or cream of mushroom soup, undiluted
1/2 cup Burgundy or sherry wine

Cube meat into bite-size pieces. Mix all ingredients
in a casserole till blended. Cover and bake at 325
degrees for 3 hours. Serve over rice or noodles.

Serves 6   Preparation time: 10 minutes

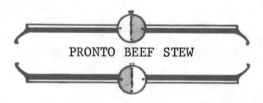

PRONTO BEEF STEW

When you are called upon to provide instant victuals...
try this!

2 tbs. butter or margarine
1/2 cup chopped frozen or fresh onion
Pinch of thyme
1 bay leaf
1 cup Burgundy wine
2 tbs. flour
1 large can beef stew
1 small can mushrooms, drained
1 small can pearl onions, drained

Sauté onion in butter or margarine. Add thyme, bay leaf,
Burgundy, and flour. Cook, stirring until mixture boils
and thickens. Add remaining ingredients and heat. Serve
with tossed salad and French bread.

Serves 4   Preparation time: 10 minutes

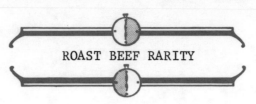

ROAST BEEF RARITY

1 sirloin tip or top round roast beef
1 or 2 cloves of garlic, put through a press
Salt
Freshly ground pepper

Rub entire roast with garlic. Sprinkle liberally with
salt and pepper. Let roast sit at room temperature
for one hour before putting in the oven. Cook uncovered
at 325 degrees for 20 minutes per pound...for medium rare.

Allow 1/2 lb. per person   Preparation time: 10 minutes

ROAST BEEF COMPLEMENT

1 cup Miracle Whip (no substitute)
2 tbs. white horseradish

Mix Miracle Whip and horseradish. Serve with thin
slices of roast beef.

Yields 1 cup   Preparation time: 5 minutes

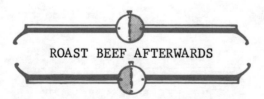

ROAST BEEF AFTERWARDS

1 cup chopped frozen or fresh onion
2 tbs. butter or margarine
1 can beef gravy
1/4 cup (or more) Burgundy wine

Sauté onion in butter or margarine. Add gravy and
Burgundy. Heat. Pour over leftover slices of roast
beef.

Yields 1 1/2 cups   Preparation time: 10 minutes

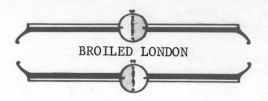

BROILED LONDON

A special favorite of mine.

1 flank steak
Meat tenderizer
1/2 bottle 1890 French dressing (no substitute)

Sprinkle tenderizer on both sides of beef and prick both sides with fork. Pour 1890 dressing over meat and marinate at room temperature for 1 hour, turning meat once. Grill or broil 5 minutes on each side or as desired.

Serves 4   Preparation time: 5 minutes

HADLY BARBECUE SAUCE

Great for hamburger, steak, or sandwich steaks.

1/2 cup (1 stick) margarine
1 small bottle A-1 sauce
1 small bottle Worcestershire sauce
1 clove garlic, minced or put through a press

Melt margarine and add rest of ingredients. Heat and stir.

Yields 2 cups   Preparation time: 5 minutes

BONANZA BARBECUE SAUCE

Great on pork chops, pork tenderloin, or pork roast.

1 cup tomato soup, undiluted
1/2 package onion soup mix

Mix ingredients together.

Yields 1 cup   Preparation time: 5 minutes

MEXICAN FIESTA CASSEROLE

2 lbs. ground beef
1 package Taco seasoning
1 package corn chips
1 cup grated sharp cheddar cheese (optional)

Brown ground beef; drain. Add Taco seasoning, according to directions on package. Spread bottom of a casserole with 1/2 the package of chips. Then add meat mixture and top with remaining chips. Grated cheese may be sprinkled on top. Bake at 350 degrees till hot - about 25 minutes. Great to prepare a day ahead, but add the chips on top just before heating.

Serves 6-8   Preparation time: 15 minutes

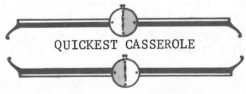

QUICKEST CASSEROLE

When you thawed hamburger in the a.m., and it is now 5 o'clock...try this.

1 lb. ground beef
1 cup chopped frozen or fresh onion
3 cups egg noodles, uncooked
3 cups tomato or V-8 juice
1 tsp. salt
1 1/2 tsp. celery salt
Dash pepper
2 tsp. Worcestershire sauce
1/2 cup frozen or fresh chopped green pepper
1 cup sour cream
1 small can mushrooms, drained

Brown beef. Add onion and noodles. Pour on next 5 ingredients. Bring to boil. Turn heat down. Cover pan and simmer, very slowly for 20 minutes. Add green pepper, cover, and continue cooking 10 minutes more or until noodles are done. Stir in sour cream and mushrooms. Heat just till it bubbles.

Serves 4-6   Preparation time: 15 minutes

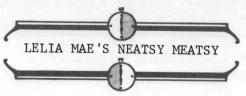

LELIA MAE'S NEATSY MEATSY

1 lb. ground beef
1 clove garlic, put through a press
1 tsp. sugar
1 tsp. salt
Dash pepper
2 8 oz. cans tomato sauce
1 8 oz. package egg noodles
1 3 oz. package cream cheese
1/2 cup chopped frozen or fresh onion
1 cup sour cream
1/2 cup grated cheddar cheese

Combine beef with next 4 ingredients. Brown beef, then
drain. Add tomato sauce. Cook egg noodles according
to directions on package, drain. Mix cream cheese,
onion, and sour cream. Place layer of noodles in a
casserole; cover with cream cheese mixture, then meat
sauce. Repeat layers. Top with cheese. Bake at 350
degrees for 30 minutes.

Serves 6   Preparation time: 25 minutes

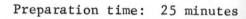

SWISH MEAT LOAF

2 lbs. ground beef
1 package onion soup mix, dry
1 cup Burgundy or red wine
1 cup tomato juice
3 strips bacon, raw
2 tbs. cornstarch (optional)

Mix meat, soup mix, 1/2 cup wine, and 1/2 cup tomato
juice. Shape into loaf. Place in pan and top with
bacon strips. Bake at 350 degrees for 45 minutes.
Drain off fat; add remaining wine and tomato juice.
Bake and baste 15 minutes longer. If desired, thicken
pan juices slightly with a little cornstarch mixed with
cold water or additional wine.

Serves 6-8   Preparation time: 15 minutes

CHICO'S SPECIAL

A ten year old can "Chef" this.

1 lb. ground beef
1 can "BIG JOHN'S beans'n fixin's"
1/2 cup grated cheddar cheese (optional)

Brown beef; drain. Add beans, heat and serve. Grated cheese may be added 5 minutes before serving.

Serves 4   Preparation time: 10 minutes

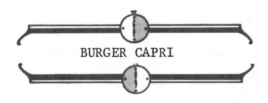

BURGER CAPRI

When the kids barge in famished, your spouse arrives home holloweyed, and you've had the Cub den all afternoon...try this!

1 lb. ground beef
1/2 tsp. salt
1/4 tsp. pepper
1 cup canned stewed tomatoes, well drained
1/2 cup grated sharp cheddar cheese
1 tsp. Italian seasoning (or oregano and basil)

Combine beef with salt and pepper. Pat beef out in 9 inch pie plate, crust fashion. Spread with tomatoes and sprinkle with remaining ingredients. Bake at 375 degrees for 25 minutes. Drain off any fat after removing from oven. Cut into wedges. May be prepared ahead of time and refrigerated until ready for cooking.

Serves 4   Preparation time: 5 minutes

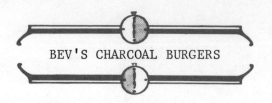

BEV'S CHARCOAL BURGERS

2 lbs. ground beef
1/2 cup chopped frozen or fresh onion
1/2 cup chopped frozen or fresh green pepper
3 tbs. white horseradish
Ketchup
Mustard

Combine first four ingredients. Shape into patties,
adding just enough ketchup and mustard to make moist.
Chill patties well before charcoaling. May be pan
fried too.

Serves 6-8   Preparation time: 15 minutes

RANCH ZEEK AND BEV BURGER

Invite the neighborhood kids over for these Ranch
Burgers. They'll never forget them.

1 lb. ground beef
1 tsp. salt
Dash pepper
3 hot dogs
4 slices American cheese
4 hamburger buns

Add salt and pepper to ground beef and shape into
patties. Pan fry or grill patties on both sides;
grill hot dogs. Split hot dogs lengthwise; then
crosswise. Place burgers on split hamburger buns.
Top each burger with 3 sections of hot dog, then 1
piece of cheese. Place under broiler until cheese
has melted. Top with other bun half before serving.

Serves 4   Preparation time: 15 minutes

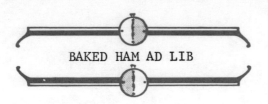

BAKED HAM AD LIB

Baste whole or 1/2 ham about every 30 minutes for 1 hour before it's ready to be taken from oven. If you use 1/2 ham, cover cut end with foil to prevent drying.

Spiced Your Choice

Honey-orange Mix 1 cup thawed frozen orange juice (undiluted) with 3/4 cup honey and 1 tsp. Worcestershire sauce. Score ham deeply into 1 inch squares before brushing with glaze.

Southern style Combine 1 cup firmly packed brown sugar, 1 tsp. dry mustard, 1/4 tsp. ground cloves, and 2 tbs. vinegar in a bowl. Score ham and stud with whole cloves before spreading with mixture.

Curry currant Mix 1 cup currant jelly with 2 tbs. hot water; stir in 2 tbs. prepared mustard, 1/4 tsp. ground cloves, and 1/4 tsp. curry.

Mustard ease Spread scored top with 1/4 cup prepared mustard, pour 1/4 cup light corn syrup over; brush with additional 1/2 cup light corn syrup until golden; sprinkle top lightly with salted peanuts.

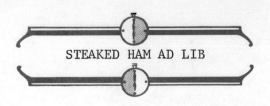

STEAKED HAM AD LIB

Ham steaks are usually 1/2 to 3/4 inch thick. Score fat edges 1 inch apart before cooking; bake at 325 degrees 30 minutes for each 3/4 inch thickness.

Spiced Your Choice

<u>Ginger-orange</u> Rub ham steak with 1/8 tsp. ground ginger and 1/8 tsp. allspice; spread with mixture of 1/4 cup orange marmalade and 1 tsp. sweet pickle juice.

<u>Chutney</u> Brush ham steak with 1 tsp. prepared mustard, then with 2 tbs. chutney (from jar).

<u>Hawaiian</u> Rub ham steak well with mixture of 2 tbs. brown sugar and 1/4 tsp. ground cloves; top with 1 can (8 oz.) crushed pineapple. Just before serving, sprinkle with coconut.

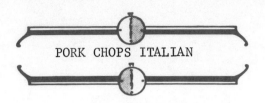

PORK CHOPS ITALIAN

1 envelope Italian dressing mix
1 cup water
1/4 cup Rose wine
6 thick pork chops (3 lbs.)

In jar combine dressing mix, water, and wine. Shake.
Pour over pork chops and marinate at room temperature,
30 minutes, turning once. Drain chops, reserving
marinade. Grill over medium low coals 15 minutes
on each side. Brush with marinade, occasionally.

Serves 4-6   Preparation time: 10 minutes

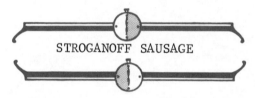

STROGANOFF SAUSAGE

A great brunch idea!

1 lb. spicy sausage (bulk)
1/2 cup chopped frozen or fresh onion
1 can cream of chicken soup (undiluted)
1/2 pint sour cream

Sauté sausage; add onion and drain. Add soup. May
be made the day ahead or morning of. Just before
serving, add sour cream and heat. Serve over rice.

Serves 6   Preparation time: 15 minutes

SAUSAGE APPLES

4 apples
1/2 lb. sausage

Core apples and stuff holes with sausage. Bake at
350 degrees for 35 minutes.

Serves 4   Preparation time: 10 minutes

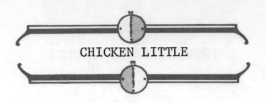

CHICKEN LITTLE

4 chicken breasts
4 chicken legs
1 package Pepperidge Farm dressing mix
1/2 pint sour cream

Dry chicken with paper towel. Rub with sour cream, covering completely. With a rolling pin, crush dressing mix into smaller pieces. Roll chicken in crushed dressing. Bake at 350 degrees for 1 hour and 15 minutes or until tender.

Serves 4   Preparation time: 15 minutes

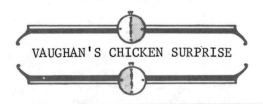

VAUGHAN'S CHICKEN SURPRISE

4 chicken breasts
4 chicken legs
1 cup chopped frozen onion or 1 fresh onion, sliced
Shortening or margarine
Salt and pepper to taste
Flour

Place chicken in pan; sprinkle onion, salt and pepper over it. Now sprinkle flour over chicken and dot with shortening or margarine. Bake at 425 degrees for 45 minutes.

Serves 4   Preparation time: 10 minutes

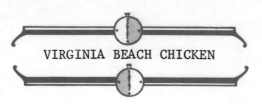

VIRGINIA BEACH CHICKEN

8 double chicken breasts, boned (if desired)
1 large jar chipped beef
8 strips bacon, raw
1/2 pint sour cream
1 can golden mushroom soup, undiluted
1/4 cup dry sherry (optional)
1 small can mushrooms, drained (optional)

Wrap each chicken breast in bacon. Pull apart chipped beef, place in bottom of casserole. Put bacon-wrapped chicken on top of beef. Combine sour cream, soup, sherry, and mushrooms and pour over all. Bake uncovered 2 hours at 300 degrees.

Serves 8-12   Preparation time: 10 minutes

CHIKIBAKE

6 strips bacon, raw
4 chicken breasts
4 chicken legs
2/3 cup rice, uncooked
1 1/3 cups stewed tomatoes, undrained
Italian seasonings or red pepper flakes
1 small can mushrooms, drained (optional)

Cover the bottom of a casserole with strips of bacon and arrange chicken pieces, skin side up, on the bacon, leaving a space in the center. Fill space with rice; cover rice with stewed tomatoes. Add your favorite Italian seasonings or red pepper flakes. Also, add mushrooms, if desired. Cover and bake at 350 degrees for 1 1/2 hours. Uncover and continue baking until the rice has absorbed all the moisture.

Serves 4   Preparation time: 15 minutes

CHICKEN DUCHESS

Leftover stuffing
2 cans Swanson's chicken a la king
2 tbs. sherry (optional)

Put half of leftover stuffing in a loaf pan or casserole.
Top with chicken à la king, then rest of stuffing.
Sherry may be added to the chicken before adding to
casserole. Bake at 325 degrees for 35 minutes.

Serves 6   Preparation time: 10 minutes

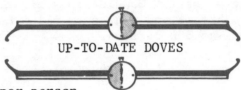

UP-TO-DATE DOVES

2 or 3 doves per person
Salt and pepper to taste
1 tbs. currant jelly per dove

Season doves with salt and pepper, inside and out.
Form aluminum foil around each dove, breast side up,
in roasting pan, leaving foil open. Place jelly on
breast of each bird. Roast for 40 minutes at 400
degrees.

                          Preparation time: 10 minutes

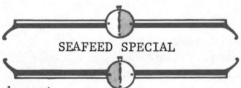

SEAFEED SPECIAL

1 lb. lump crab meat
2/3 cup mayonnaise
1/3 cup Durkee's salad dressing
1/2 tsp. Lawry's seasoned salt
12 Ritz crackers, crumbled

Blend; put in buttered casserole. Sprinkle crumbled
crackers over top. Dot with butter. Bake at 350
degrees for 25 minutes.

Serves 4   Preparation time: 10 minutes

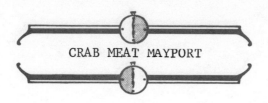

CRAB MEAT MAYPORT

1 can cream of celery soup, undiluted
1/4 cup water
1 tbs. dry white wine
2 7 oz. cans King crab meat
1 tbs. chopped parsley
1/2 cup grated sharp cheddar cheese
1 cup bread crumbs

Blend soup and water with wine. Pick through crab meat carefully to remove shell. Mix in crab and parsley. Pour into individual shells or casserole. Top with cheese and crumbs. Bake at 400 degrees for 20 minutes.

Serves 4   Preparation time: 20 minutes

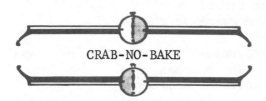

CRAB-NO-BAKE

Serve this as an entrée, or as an appetizer with Melba toast.

1 8 oz. package cream cheese (at room temperature for
    1 hour)
1/2 pint sour cream
2 tbs. lemon juice
2 tbs. sherry
1 envelope Italian dressing mix
1 lb. crab meat

The day before serving, combine all ingredients. In summer serve cold in individual shells. Also nice as a cold dip or hot, in a chafing dish.

Serves 4   Preparation time: 15 minutes

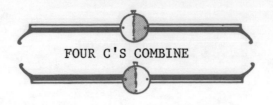

FOUR C'S COMBINE

(CINN'S CRAB AND CORN COMBINATION)

When economy is more important than time, feed 4 on
1 can of crab meat.

1 6-1/2 oz. can crab meat or 1 cup fresh crab
1 16 oz. can whole-kernel corn
3 shelled hard cooked eggs, chopped
1 tbs. chopped parsley
2 tsp. lemon juice
1 tbs. chopped frozen or fresh onion
3 tbs. margarine or butter
2 tbs. flour
1 tsp. dry mustard
1 cup milk
1/2 tsp. salt
1/2 tsp. Worcestershire sauce
1 tbs. margarine or butter
1/2 cup bread crumbs
1/4 cup grated Parmesan cheese

In 1 1/2 quart casserole, toss crab meat with next 4
ingredients. In saucepan, cook onion in 3 tbs. margarine or butter for 3 minutes; stir in flour, mustard,
then milk. Cook, stirring until thickened. Add salt
and Worcestershire sauce. Turn into casserole; toss
with fork. Melt 1 tbs. margarine or butter, stir in
crumbs and cheese. Sprinkle crumb mixture on top.
Chill casserole. Let sit at room temperature 40 minutes before baking at 375 degrees for 20-25 minutes.

Serves 4   Preparation time: 30 minutes

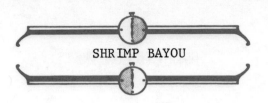

SHRIMP BAYOU

4 tbs. bacon drippings
1 cup chopped frozen or fresh onion
1/2 cup chopped frozen or fresh green pepper
1 1/2 cups chopped celery
1 quart can tomatoes, drained
3 tbs. tomato paste
1 tbs. sugar
Salt and pepper to taste
3 cups cooked shrimp, fresh or flash frozen (1 lb.)

Sauté onion, green pepper, and celery in bacon drippings until soft. Add remaining ingredients except shrimp. Let mixture simmer to a thick consistency about 30 minutes. Ten minutes before serving, add cooked shrimp. Serve over rice.

Serves 6   Preparation time: 25 minutes

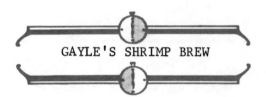

GAYLE'S SHRIMP BREW

Each guest peels his own shrimp and loves it.

5 lbs. unpeeled shrimp (fresh or flash frozen)
4 cans beer
1 pint vinegar
1/2 cup salt
1/4 cup pepper
1/8 cup cayenne
Melted butter

Combine all ingredients except melted butter. Boil shrimp in liquid for 5 minutes. Put an empty plate for shells in front of every two guests. Serve each guest a small dish of hot melted butter in which he dips his shrimp.

Serves 6   Preparation time: 5 minutes

GOLDEN CHEESE GRITS

1 1/4 cup grits, uncooked
3 1/2 cups boiling water
1 roll cheese or bacon-flavored cheese
1/2 cup (1 stick) butter
2 eggs
1 cup milk

Preheat oven to 350 degrees. Cook grits in boiling
water, according to directions on package. Crumble
cheese and butter into cooked grits. Blend eggs
and milk together. Mix with grits. Pour mixture
into a greased 2-quart casserole. Bake at 350 degrees
for 1 hour, uncovered.

Serves 8   Preparation time: 20 minutes

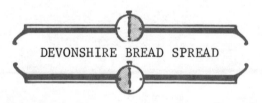

DEVONSHIRE BREAD SPREAD

Great sandwich for Saturday lunches, or as supper
sandwich with soup.

8 strips bacon
4 English muffin halves, toasted
1 jar sandwich spread
4 slices of tomato
4 Swiss cheese slices

Fry bacon, drain. Spread toasted muffin halves with
sandwich spread. On each half, place slice of
tomato, 2 bacon strips, then top with cheese. Bake
at 350 degrees till cheese melts.

Yields 4 open-faced sandwiches

                    Preparation time: 15 minutes

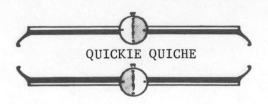

QUICKIE QUICHE

1 prepared frozen pie shell
4 eggs
1 cup milk
Salt and pepper to taste
4 slices ham, diced
3 slices Swiss cheese, diced

Put ham and cheese in bottom of pie shell. Beat
eggs with milk, salt, and pepper. Pour egg mixture
on top. Bake at 375 degrees for 30 minutes till
eggs are set and brown on top.

Serves 4   Preparation time: 10 minutes

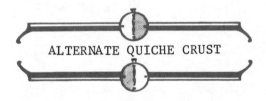

ALTERNATE QUICHE CRUST

3 oz. cream cheese, softened
1/2 cup (1 stick) margarine or butter
1 1/4 cup flour

Mix ingredients and shape into ball. Press into an
8" by 8" by 2" pie plate.

Yields one pie crust   Preparation time: 10 minutes

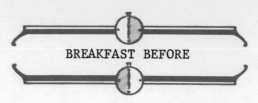

BREAKFAST BEFORE

Make on Saturday, refrigerate, then pop in the oven
45 minutes before serving for Sunday brunch.

1 lb. spicy pork sausage (bulk)
6 eggs
2 cups milk
1 tsp. salt
1 tsp. dry mustard
2 slices white bread, cubed
1 cup grated sharp cheddar cheese

Sauté sausage; drain. Beat eggs with milk, salt, and
mustard. Layer the bread cubes, sausage, and cheese
in a 9" by 13" baking dish. Pour egg mixture on top.
Refrigerate overnight. Bake at 350 degrees for 45
minutes.

Serves 6-8   Preparation time: 20 minutes

PIZZA POACH

2 eggs per person
1 can pizza sauce
Evaporated milk

Pour pizza sauce and dilute with enough evaporated
milk to make 1/2 inch liquid in bottom of small fry-
ing pan. Bring to boil and drop in raw eggs, spoon-
ing sauce over eggs.

                              Preparation time: 10 minutes

Varieties of the Garden

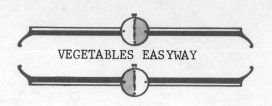

VEGETABLES EASYWAY

Why not use your oven to best advantage? While your entrée is cooking, break up a package of frozen vegetables (except for chopped spinach and chopped broccoli) and gently separate by letting water run over the vegetables. Season with salt, pepper, MSG, and butter. Add a pinch of sugar or herbs; if you like. Wrap in foil and bake, seam side up, at 350 degrees (see timetable below). The vegetables steam in their own juices, are delicious, and better for you. Also, there's no pan to wash.

Cooking vegetables in foil at 350 degrees

Chopped spinach, defrosted........35-40 minutes
Chopped broccoli, defrosted.......35-40 minutes
Green beans......................40 minutes
Cauliflower......................30 minutes
Brussel sprouts..................40-50 minutes
Broccoli spears..................50 minutes
Asparagus spears.................40 minutes
Lima beans (add 2 tbs. water).....1 hour, 15 minutes
Peas.............................30 minutes

Preparation time: 5 minutes

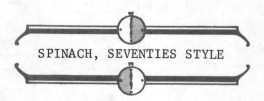

SPINACH, SEVENTIES STYLE

2 packages frozen chopped spinach, defrosted and
    drained
1 cup sour cream
1 envelope onion soup mix

Combine all ingredients and bake in tightly covered casserole at 350 degrees for 30 minutes.

Serves 6   Preparation time: 5 minutes

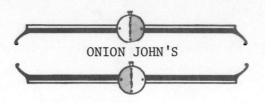

ONION JOHN'S

6 medium yellow onions
Butter
Salt and pepper to taste

Do not peel, leave completely intact. Place onions
in foil in a 350 degree oven for 1 1/2 hours. Treat
onion like a baked potato. When very soft, remove
to platter, split open lengthwise, and season with
butter, salt, and pepper to taste.

Serves 6   Preparation time: 5 minutes

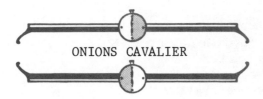

ONIONS CAVALIER

A great accompaniment to roast beef!

5 onions, sliced 1/2 inch thick
1/2 tsp. MSG
1/2 tsp. sugar
1/2 tsp. salt
1/2 tsp. pepper
1/3 cup butter or margarine
1/2 cup sherry
2 tbs. Parmesan cheese

Season sliced onions with MSG, sugar, salt, and pepper.
Sauté in butter 5-8 minutes or till barely tender,
stirring to separate rings. Add sherry; cook quickly
2 or 3 minutes. Sprinkle with cheese.

Serves 6   Preparation time: 15 minutes

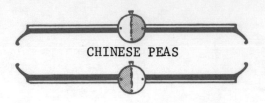

CHINESE PEAS

2 packages frozen Chinese peas (snow peas)
2 cans chicken broth

Substituting broth for water, cook according to
directions.

Serves 4-6   Preparation time: 5 minutes

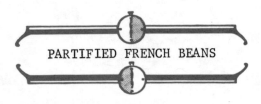

PARTIFIED FRENCH BEANS

2 packages frozen French cut beans
1 can cream of mushroom or cream of vegetable soup
1/4 tsp. dry mustard
1/4 tsp. thyme
1/2 tsp. seasoned salt
1/2 cup milk (or part sherry)
1 6 oz. can water chestnuts, drained and sliced
1 cup grated cheddar cheese
1 can French fried onions

Cook beans according to directions until tender; drain.
Place in shallow casserole. Combine with remaining
ingredients except cheese and French fried onions.
Bake at 350 degrees for 20 minutes. Sprinkle on onions
and cheese and bake 10 more minutes.

Serves 4-6   Preparation time: 15 minutes

SOUL PEAS

Black-eyed peas are a real favorite at our house.
This is my quick version.

2 strips bacon
1 cup chopped frozen or fresh onions
1 bay leaf
1/2 tsp. garlic powder
Sprinkling of red pepper flakes (optional)
1 can black-eyed peas

Fry bacon in saucepan. Add onion, seasonings, then
peas. Simmer 10 to 15 minutes.

Serves 2-3   Preparation time: 10 minutes

ENGLISH PEA CASSEROLE

2 cans Le Seur peas, drained
1 cup chopped celery
1 cup water chestnuts, drained and sliced
1 can cream of celery soup
1/2 cup chopped frozen or fresh onion
2 tbs. chopped frozen or fresh green pepper
3 tbs. chopped pimento (optional)

Combine all ingredients and bake at 350 degrees until
heated through.

Serves 6   Preparation time: 15 minutes

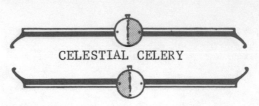

CELESTIAL CELERY

When you are serving an instant entrée, for instance, Gayle's Shrimp Brew (a 5 minute preparation time dish), fix this the day before your dinner party.

4 cups celery, scraped, then sliced on the diagonal
    in 1 inch pieces
1/4 cup chopped frozen or fresh onion
1/2 cup chopped frozen or fresh green pepper
2 tbs. butter or margarine
1 small package cream cheese, at room temperature
2 small packages blue cheese, at room temperature
1 cup heavy cream
Slivered almonds
Paprika

Cook celery in water till tender but still crisp (approximately 5 minutes). Drain in collander and rinse with cold water. Sauté onion and pepper in butter or margarine. Stir in cream cheese, blue cheese, and cream. Mix till smooth. Add celery and mix all ingredients except almonds and paprika. Put mixture in casserole. Bake at 350 degrees until hot -- about 20 minutes. Sprinkle with almonds the last 10 minutes. Garnish with paprika.

Serves 6   Preparation time: 30 minutes

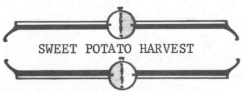

SWEET POTATO HARVEST

1 can sweet potatoes
1 can sliced apples
1 jar spiced peaches, juice
1 tsp. cinnamon sugar
1 package mini-marshmallows

Layer potatoes, as you slice them, with apples and peaches. Pour enough spiced peach juice over mixture to moisten well. Sprinkle with cinnamon sugar and top with marshmallows. Bake at 350 degrees until hot and and marshmallows begin to brown - about 30 minutes.

Serves 6-8   Preparation time: 10 minutes

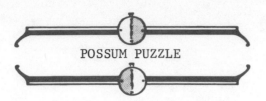

POSSUM PUZZLE

This conversation piece will fool you and puzzle your
most alert guest.

1   10 oz. can tomato puree
1/4 cup water
1/4 tsp. salt
2/3 cup brown sugar
6 slices bread
1/2 cup (1 stick) butter, melted

Bring tomato puree and water to a boil. Remove from
heat and add salt and brown sugar. Remove crusts from
bread, break into small pieces, and place in buttered
casserole. Add melted butter and tomato puree mixture.
Cover and bake at 350 degrees for 1 hour. Let stand
uncovered 5 minutes before serving with meat course.

Serves 6-8   Preparation time: 25 minutes

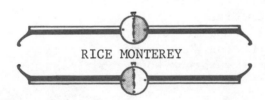

RICE MONTEREY

1 cup hot rice (cooked with salt)
2 cups grated Monterey Jack cheese
1 pint sour cream
Salt to taste
1 small can ortega chilies (green chilies)

Mix all of the ingredients while rice is hot, to
blend easily. Pour into buttered casserole. Bake
for 30 minutes at 350 degrees. Brown under broiler.

Serves 6   Preparation time: 20 minutes

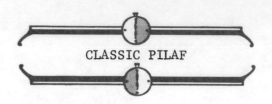

CLASSIC PILAF

1 1/3 cups precooked rice
1 can onion soup, undiluted
1 2 oz. can sliced mushrooms, undrained
1/3 cup Sauterne
1 tbs. chopped parsley

Combine all ingredients. Heat to boiling. Remove
from heat, cover, let stand 5 minutes.

Serves 4   Preparation time: 5 minutes

BROCCOLI AND RICE MAGNIFIQUE

2 packages frozen chopped broccoli, defrosted
2 cups cooked rice
1 cup frozen or fresh chopped onion
1 cup chopped celery
3 tbs. plus 1/2 cup (1 stick) butter or margarine
1 8 oz. jar Cheese Whiz
2 cans cream of mushroom soup, undiluted

Sauté onion and celery in 3 tbs. butter. Add remaining ingredients. Mix and pour in casserole. Bake at
350 degrees for 45 minutes.

Serves 6-8   Preparation time: 20 minutes

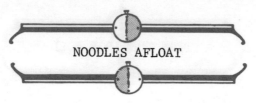

NOODLES AFLOAT

2 tbs. basil
2 tbs. parsley
1/4 cup (1/2 stick) softened butter
1 clove garlic, put through a press
2/3 cup boiling water
1 8 oz. package cream cheese
1/3 cup grated Parmesan cheese
1/4 cup olive or salad oil
1/2 tsp. pepper
1 large package flat egg noodles, cooked and drained

Put all ingredients, except noodles, in saucepan and
bring to a boil. Place noodles in casserole and pour
sauce over all. Bake 15 minutes at 350 degrees.

Serves 6-8   Preparation time: 20 minutes

NOODLE DOODLE & CHEESE

Super good!

5 cans macaroni and cheese sauce
1 package frozen chopped spinach or broccoli,
    defrosted and drained
1 small bunch green onions, cut finely
1/2 tsp. oregano
1 can French fried onions
1/2 lb. grated sharp cheddar cheese

In a 3 quart casserole, mix all ingredients together
except for the French fried onions and a small portion
of the cheese. Refrigerate. When ready to bake, top
casserole with French fried onions and the remaining
cheese. Bake uncovered at 350 degrees for 45 to 60
minutes, till hot and bubbly.

Serves 8   Preparation time: 20 minutes

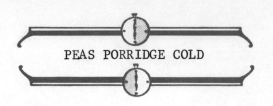

PEAS PORRIDGE COLD

1 10 oz. package frozen peas
1/4 cup chopped frozen or fresh onion
1 tsp. white horseradish
2 tbs. sour cream
Bibb or Boston lettuce

Cook peas with onions. Drain and chill. Blend
horseradish and sour cream. Gently fold in peas.
Refrigerate. Serve cold on lettuce leaves.

Serves 2-3   Preparation time: 15 minutes

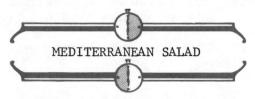

MEDITERRANEAN SALAD

1 16 oz. can or jar whole carrots, drained
1 fresh zucchini, thinly sliced
1 14 oz. can hearts of palm, drained and cut in
     thick slices
2/3 cup salad oil
1/4 cup vinegar
1 small clove of garlic, minced
1 tsp. sugar
3/4 tsp. salt
3/4 tsp. dry mustard
Dash freshly ground pepper
1 head Bibb lettuce (if not available, use a different
     variety)
1 2 oz. package blue cheese, crumbled

In shallow dish, combine carrots, zucchini, and
hearts of palm. In a jar, combine oil, vinegar,
garlic, sugar, salt, mustard, and pepper, and shake
well. Pour over vegetables. Chill several hours,
preferably over night. To serve, drain off marinade,
arrange on lettuce, and top with cheese.

Serves 6-8   Preparation time: 10 minutes

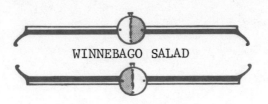

WINNEBAGO SALAD

1 jar marinated artichokes, undrained
1 jar marinated mushrooms, undrained
1 lb. jar sweet and sour vegetable salad, drained
    (contains green, wax, kidney, and lima beans,
    carrots, celery, onions, etc.)
1 head of romaine, broken in pieces
1 avocado, sliced (optional)

Toss and serve.

Serves 6   Preparation time: 10 minutes

AVOCADO ASPIC

1 small package raspberry-flavored gelatin
2 cups hot tomato juice
1 tbs. white horseradish
1 7-3/4 oz. can frozen avocado dip, defrosted
Coleslaw dressing (optional)

Dissolve gelatin in tomato juice. Pour in bottom of
1 pint mold a small amount of gelatin mixture and chill
until slightly firm. Mix horseradish and frozen
avocado dip and spread on mold. Cover with remaining
gelatin and refrigerate to jell. Pour coleslaw dressing
over, if desired.

Serves 6   Preparation time: 10 minutes

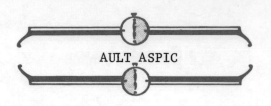

AULT ASPIC

1 can (1 lb.) stewed tomatoes
1 small package raspberry-flavored gelatin
3/4 cup boiling water
3 to 4 drops Tabasco sauce
Mayonnaise
Coleslaw dressing

Break up tomatoes with a spoon. Dissolve gelatin in water; add Tabasco sauce and tomatoes. Turn into individual molds greased with mayonnaise; refrigerate until firm. Mixture congeals in 1 hour. Unmold and serve with coleslaw dressing.

Serves 4-6   Preparation time: 10 minutes

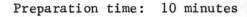

APPLESAUCE REVEL

1 small can applesauce
1 small package raspberry-flavored gelatin
1 small bottle ginger ale
2 tsp. white horseradish
Mayonnaise

Heat applesauce until bubbly. Stir in gelatin. Add ginger ale and horseradish. Grease individual molds with mayonnaise and fill with applesauce mixture. Refrigerate until set.

Serves 6   Preparation time: 10 minutes

LE MANDARIN ORANGE

1 large package orange-flavored gelatin
1 medium can crushed pineapple
1 can mandarin oranges
1 pint sour cream
1 package mini-marshmallows

Make gelatin according to directions, substituting
juice from pineapple and oranges for part of water.
Add fruit, and pour into a 9" by 13" casserole.
Refrigerate. When congealed, cover gelatin dessert
with marshmallows. Then spread sour cream over
marshmallows.

Serves 8   Preparation time: 15 minutes

FIESTA FRUIT FREEZE

1 large can fruit cocktail, drained
1 can mandarin oranges, drained
1/2 cup chopped maraschino cherries (optional)
1/2 cup pecans, chopped
2 bananas, sliced
1 large container Cool Whip
Mayonnaise

Mix all fruit together; then add nuts and fold in
Cool Whip. Put mixture in mold greased with mayonnaise,
or divide among muffin paper cups and place in muffin
tin until frozen. Once frozen, remove individual
salads and place in plastic bags. Keep in freezer
and take out as many as you need at a time.

Serves 8   Preparation time: 10 minutes

CRANBERRY ORANGE RELISH

1 orange
2 cups raw cranberries
3/4 cup sugar

Quarter the unpeeled oranges. Remove seeds, grind
orange to a fine pulp in blender at low speed. Add
1 cup cranberries and run at low speed to a coarse
grind. Empty container. Process the second cup of
cranberries. Add sugar to cranberries. Mix throughly.
Refrigerate.

Yields 2 cups   Preparation time: 10 minutes

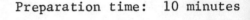

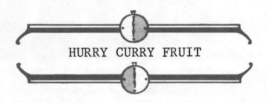

HURRY CURRY FRUIT

When company is expected and you want one special
addition, this is perfect!

1 cup light brown sugar
3 tsp. curry powder
1/2 cup (1 stick) butter, melted
1 large can pineapple chunks, drained
1 large can peaches, drained
1 large can pears, drained
1 can mandarin oranges, drained

Place drained fruits in a casserole. Combine sugar
and curry powder. Add to melted butter and spoon
over fruits. Bake at 350 degrees for 1 hour. Serve
warm.

May be made the day before and reheated just before
serving.

Serves 6-8   Preparation time: 10 minutes

Smashing Sweets

PIE MAGIC

1/2 cup chopped pecans
1 7-1/2 oz. jar chocolate fudge topping
1 large carton Cool Whip
1 frozen pie shell, baked according to directions
Chocolate shavings

Fold pecans and chocolate into Cool Whip. Pile into
baked pie shell and refrigerate. Garnish with shaved
chocolate before serving. Butterscotch, strawberry,
or pineapple topping may be substituted for chocolate
topping.

Serves 6   Preparation time: 10 minutes

FUDGE PIE

1 cup sugar
1/2 cup (1 stick) margarine or butter
2 eggs
1 package choco-bake, melted
1/2 cup flour
1 tsp. vanilla
1/2 cup chopped pecans
Cool Whip (optional)
1 quart ice cream (optional)

Mix sugar and margarine or butter. Beat in eggs; add
melted choco-bake. Beat in flour; add vanilla and
chopped pecans. Bake in greased pie plate at 325
degrees for 30 minutes. Slice in wedges and top with
vanilla ice cream or Cool Whip.

Serves 6   Preparation time: 10 minutes

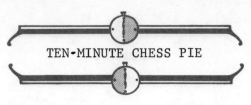

TEN-MINUTE CHESS PIE

1/2 cup (1 stick) butter, not margarine
1 cup sugar
1 tbs. yellow cornmeal
3 eggs
1/3 cup fresh lemon juice, rind of 1 lemon
1 frozen unbaked pie shell

Cream sugar and butter; add cornmeal. Beat in each
egg individually; add lemon rind and juice. Pour
mixture into pie shell. Bake at 375 degrees for
25 to 30 minutes.

Serves 6   Preparation time: 10 minutes

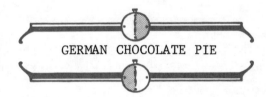

GERMAN CHOCOLATE PIE

Crust

2 egg whites
1/8 tsp. salt
1/8 tsp. cream of tartar
1/2 cup sugar
1/2 tsp. vanilla
1/2 cup finely chopped walnuts

Beat egg whites till stiff. Beat in remaining ingredients
except walnuts. Add nuts; then fold mixture into lightly
greased pie tin. Bake at 300 degrees for 50-55 minutes.

Filling

1 bar German chocolate
4 tbs. water
1 tbs. vanilla
1/2 pint whipping cream
Chocolate shavings

Melt German chocolate. Add 4 tbs. water -- let cool.
Add 1 tbs. vanilla to chocolate. Whip cream and fold
into chocolate. Pile in shell and chill. Shave chocolate on top.

Serves 6   Preparation time: 15 minutes

COCKTAIL PIE

1 frozen pie shell
1 1 lb. 14 oz. can fruit cocktail, drained
1 pint sour cream
Nutmeg

Mix fruits and sour cream, place in pie shell, and
bake 20 minutes at 350 degrees. Chill. Serve with
sprinkled nutmeg as garnish.

Serves 6   Preparation time: 10 minutes

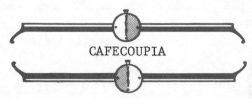

CAFECOUPIA

The aroma of this recipe carries with it the nostalgia
of all the past years of good Virginia eating.

1 lb. pork sausage, spicy or regular
1 1/2 cups firmly packed brown sugar
1 1/2 cups granulated sugar
2 eggs, lightly beaten
3 cups sifted flour
1 tsp. ginger
1 tsp. baking powder
1 tsp. pumpkin pie spice
1 tsp. baking soda
1 cup strong coffee
1 cup raisins
1 cup chopped walnuts

In mixing bowl, combine meat and sugars and stir until
mixture is well blended. Add eggs and beat well. Mix
flour, ginger, baking powder, and pumpkin pie spice.
Stir baking soda into coffee. Add flour mixture and
coffee alternately to meat mixture, beating well after
each addition. Pour boiling water over raisins, and
let stand 5 minutes; drain well and dry raisins in
cloth. Fold raisins and walnuts into cake batter. Turn
batter into well greased and floured mini-bundt pan.

Bake 1 1/2 hours at 350 degrees. Cool 15 minutes in pan
before turning out.

Serves 16   Preparation time: 20 minutes

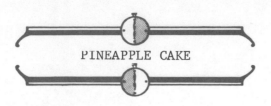

PINEAPPLE CAKE

1 package white cake mix
1 package lemon instant pudding
1 cup pineapple juice
1/2 cup salad oil
4 eggs
1 13 oz. can crushed pineapple, drained
Confectioners sugar or pineapple topping

Mix all ingredients and blend with electric beater
5 minutes. Pour into greased bundt or tube pan or
into 2 layer and bake at 350 degrees for 50 minutes
for bundt pan according to directions for layer
pans. To remove from pan sprinkle with confectioners
sugar or use pineapple topping.

Serves 16   Preparation time: 15 minutes

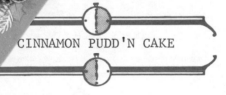

CINNAMON PUDD'N CAKE

Great for a coffee or brunch - especially
to celebrate a birthday!

1 package yellow cake mix
1 package instant vanilla or butterscotch pudding
4 eggs
1 cup water
1/2 cup (1 stick) soft margarine
1 tsp. vanilla
1/4 cup sugar
1 tsp. ground cinnamon
Confectioners sugar

Combine cake mix, pudding, eggs, water, margarine and
vanilla. Beat at medium speed with mixer for 10 minutes.
Pour into greased 10 inch tube or bundt pan. Combine
sugar and cinnamon; sprinkle over batter. Cut through
batter with spatula or knife. Bake at 350 degrees for
45 minutes. Cool in pan for 10 minutes, then sprinkle
with confectioners sugar just before serving.

Serves 16   Preparation time: 15 minutes

PUDDING FLAMBÉ

1 can plum pudding
1 tbs. orange or lemon extract
Prepared hard sauce (optional)

Preheat oven to 325 degrees. Open large end of pudding
can, leaving lid on. Cover completely with foil. Bake
about 30 minutes at 325 degrees.

For the crowning glory, once you've placed pudding on
serving dish, pour extract over pudding. Ignite with
match. Decorate with sprig and holly. If desired,
serve with prepared hard sauce.

Serves 4   Preparation time: 10 minutes

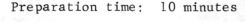

CAKE CHOCOLADA

R - Rated Rich!

1/2 cup (1 stick) margarine
1/2 cup shortening
4 tsp. cocoa
1 cup water
2 cups flour
2 cups sugar
1/2 cup buttermilk
1 tsp. baking soda
1 tsp. vanilla
2 eggs, beaten

Melt margarine, shortening, cocoa, and water; boil
rapidly. Mix flour and sugar; pour cocoa mixture
on top. Add buttermilk, soda, vanilla, and eggs.
Pour in 9" by 13" pan. Cook at 400 degrees for 30
minutes.

Serves 10   Preparation time: 25 minutes

DEMI-CHEESE CAKES MELBA

2 8 oz. packages cream cheese, softened
3/4 cup sugar
1/2 tsp. vanilla
3 eggs
1 box vanilla wafers
1 box raspberry or cherry pie filling

Mix together cream cheese, sugar, and vanilla. Beat
3 eggs and add to cream cheese mixture. Put vanilla
wafer in paper muffin cup, then place in muffin pan,
and fill each cup half full with cheese mixture. Bake
at 350 degrees for 12 minutes. After removing from
oven, add 1 or 2 spoonfuls of raspberry or cherry pie
filling on top.

Serves 12   Preparation time: 10 minutes

ANGEL FOOD SHERRY

Angel food cake, store-bought
1/2 cup sherry
1/2 pint sour cream
1 large can peach slices

Soak cake in sherry on all sides. After cake soaks
up sherry, coat cake with sour cream on all sides.
Just before serving, arrange canned peach slices on
top of cake so that each slice has a peach. Serve
a bowl of sliced peaches to be passed with cake.

Serves 6-8   Preparation time: 10 minutes

SHERRY CAKE

1 package yellow cake mix
1 small package vanilla, butterscotch, or coconut
    instant pudding
4 eggs
3/4 cup oil
3/4 cup sherry wine
1 tsp. nutmeg
Confectioners sugar

Combine all ingredients. Beat with electric beater
for 5 minutes. Pour into greased bundt or tube pan.
Bake at 350 degrees for approximately 50 minutes.
Cool in pan for 5 minutes before turning out. Sprinkle
with confectioners sugar.

Serves 16   Preparation time: 10 minutes

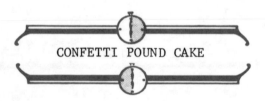

CONFETTI POUND CAKE

1 pound cake mix
1/2 cup raisins
1/2 cup chopped candied fruit
1/2 tsp. rum flavoring or
    1 tbs. rum
Confectioners sugar

Bake cake according to directions adding raisins, fruit,
and rum. Sprinkle with confectioners sugar.

Serves 6-8   Preparation time: 10 minutes

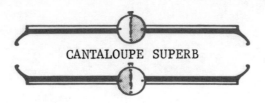

CANTALOUPE SUPERB

1 cantaloupe
1 package coconut pudding mix
Cool Whip
1 tbs. frozen coconut
1 tsp. chopped ginger

Fill 1/2 cantaloupe with coconut pudding mix, prepared according to directions. Garnish with frozen coconut, Cool Whip, and chopped ginger. Serve with Jasmine tea.

Serves 2   Preparation time: 10 minutes

WINE JELLY

A simpler recipe can't be found, and it is best made the day ahead.

1 package orange-flavored gelatin
1 package lemon-flavored gelatin
3 tbs. sugar
1/4 tsp. nutmeg
1/4 tsp. cinnamon
2 cups boiling water
1/2 cup sherry
1/2 cup orange juice
3 cups cold water
Cool Whip

Add two cups boiling water to dry ingredients and stir. Add sherry and orange juice. Add 3 cups cold water and stir. Refrigerate overnight and serve with dollop of Cool Whip on top.

Serves 10   Preparation time: 10 minutes

ICE CREAM APRICOT

1/2 gallon vanilla ice cream, softened
1/2 6 oz. can frozen lemonade concentrate,
    thawed and undiluted
1 6 oz. jar apricot preserves

Mix ingredients together and freeze.

Serves 6-8   Preparation time: 10 minutes

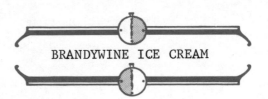

BRANDYWINE ICE CREAM

1 1/2 quarts vanilla ice cream, softened
4 1/2 oz. Blackberry brandy
3 oz. Scotch

Blend ingredients in mixer to creamy consistency.
Freeze.

Serves 8   Preparation time: 5 minutes

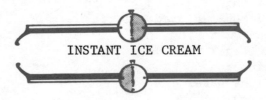

INSTANT ICE CREAM

1 quart vanilla ice cream, softened
1 or 2 cups sliced fresh strawberries, peaches, figs,
    or your choice of fresh fruit
3 tbs. rum (optional)

Combine ice cream and fresh fruit; add rum if desired.
Freeze. If you prefer fruit pureed, buzz in blender
before combining with ice cream.

Serves 6   Preparation time: 10 minutes

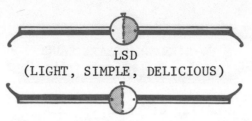

LSD
(LIGHT, SIMPLE, DELICIOUS)

This lemon ice was originally found in a cookbook for babies. It's my favorite quickie.

7 tbs. fresh lemon juice (3-4 lemons)
1 cup sugar
2 cups milk
Green Crème de Menthe (optional)

Mix sugar and lemon juice in 8" by 8" square pan or dish. Then gradually stir in milk. Freeze in pan or freezer tray. Take from freezer 5 minutes before serving. Cube with a knife, as you would fudge. Pile in dessert dish and serve with cookies. If you enjoy gilding the lily, pour a spoonful of green Crème de Menthe over each dishful.

Serves 6-8   Preparation time: 10 minutes

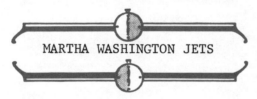

MARTHA WASHINGTON JETS

Our favorite candy! You'll have to tell guests it's homemade - it looks professional!

1 box confectioners sugar
Pinch salt
1/2 cup (1 stick) softened butter
1 tbs. vanilla
1 tbs. milk
4 packages choco-bake
Pecan chips

Gradually work sugar and salt into butter. Blend together with hand. When blended, add vanilla and milk. Work mixture into individual balls and place on waxed paper. Melt chocolate in small, deep pan. With fork, drop balls into chocolate, one at a time. Roll around until well coated; then place on waxed paper until firm and cool. Top each one with chip of pecan.

Yields 60 small candies   Preparation time: 25 minutes

NO-BAKE CHOCOLATE SAUCE

Delicious on vanilla ice cream or cake!

2 packages choco-bake
1/2 cup sugar
3 tbs. coffee
3 tbs. sherry
1/2 tsp. vanilla
Pinch salt

Blend at high speed choco-bake, sugar, coffee, sherry, vanilla, and salt. Beat for 1 minute or until very smooth. Store in refrigerator.

Serves 4-6   Preparation time: 5 minutes

CRANBERRY SAUCE

1 cup whole cranberry sauce
1/4 cup rum

Heat cranberry sauce and add rum. Serve over pound cake or pudding.

Yields 1 1/4 cups   Preparation time: 5 minutes

MINCEMEAT SAUCE

1 1/3 cup mincemeat (from jar)
1/4 cup rum

Bring mincemeat and rum to boil and remove from heat. Serve over spice cake, pound cake, or gingerbread.

Yields 1 1/2 cups   Preparation time: 5 minutes

own the Hatch: Toasts and Libations

TOASTS

I drink to the general joy of the whole table.

William Shakespeare

No poem was ever written by a drinker of water.

Horace

He who drinks, gets drunk
He who gets drunk, goes to sleep
He who goes to sleep, does not sin
He who does not sin, goes to Heaven
So let's all drink and go to Heaven.

To health, love and wealth, and the time to enjoy them.

And Noah he often said to his wife when he sat down to dine, "I don't care where the water goes if it doesn't get into the wine."

Gilbert Keith Chesterton

May you get to Heaven one-half hour before the devil knows you're gone.

A wonderful bird is the sea-gull....I'm speaking now of the he-gull....He goes on long flights for days and for nights....which is tough on his missus the she-gull.

Here's to the happy, hoppy flea
You cannot tell the he from she.
The sexes look alike, you see
But she can tell and so can he.

Your favorite toasts:

_____

_____

_____

_____

_____

_____

_____

_____

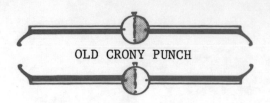

OLD CRONY PUNCH

2 12 oz. cans frozen lemonade, diluted
2 12 oz. cans frozen orange juice, diluted
1 1/2 cup maraschino cherry juice
2 fifths bourbon
2 quarts sparkling water
4 quarts ginger ale

Blend first 3 ingredients and chill. Add last 3
ingredients just before serving.

Yields 110 4 oz. servings   Preparation time: 15 minutes

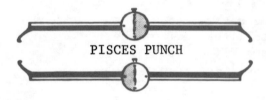

PISCES PUNCH

1 fifth bourbon
1 fifth sauterne
1 quart ginger ale
2 quarts orange sherbet

Chill all bottles. Just before guests arrive pour
bourbon and sauterne in bowl, then ginger ale. Just
before serving, add sherbet in small lumps.

Serves 18 generously   Preparation time: 10 minutes

74

DISTAFF BREW

Something for the girls.

1 quart dry sherry or sauterne
1 small can frozen lemonade, diluted

Make a day ahead if desired. Chill before serving.

Makes 16 2 oz. drinks   Preparation time: 5 minutes

RUM DUM

Make frozen lemonade according to directions.
Add dark rum to taste.

Serves 6   Preparation time: 5 minutes

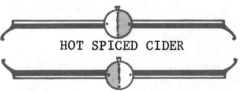

HOT SPICED CIDER

For the little folks...

2 quarts sweet cider
1 tsp. whole cloves
1 tsp. allspice
2 sticks cinnamon
1/2 cup light brown sugar, packed

Mix all ingredients together. Heat and serve.

Doctored for the big folks...

After heating to boiling point, spike with rum or
vodka to taste.

Serves 12   Preparation time: 15 minutes

CHILDREN'S SPARKLE

1 10 oz. jar mint jelly
1 cup water
2 12 oz. cans pineapple juice
1 cup water
1/2 cup lemon juice, frozen, not lemonade
1 quart ginger ale

Combine jelly with 1 cup water in saucepan. Place
over low heat and stir until jelly is melted. Cool,
add pineapple juice, one cup water, and lemon juice.
Chill. (Make ahead if desired.) Add ginger ale just
before serving.

Serves 10-12   Preparation time: 25 minutes

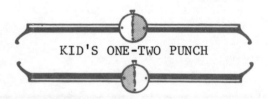

KID'S ONE-TWO PUNCH

1 can Hawaiian Punch or 1 can Hi-C
1 large bottle ginger ale

Mix ingredients and add ice.

Serves 8-10   Preparation time: 5 minutes

SANGRIA IRLANDESA

A favorite of Irish Rogues.

2 sliced oranges
2 sliced lemons
2 packages sliced frozen peaches
1/2 cup sugar
1/3 fifth cognac or brandy
Juice of 1/2 a lemon
1 fifth Burgundy
1 large bottle 7-Up

Fill a large punch bowl 1/4 full with slices of orange, lemon, and peach (frozen). Add sugar and mix well. Then add 1/3 of a fifth of cognac or brandy; spice with juice of 1/2 lemon. Allow to marinate until "congenial." At party time add equal portions of Burgundy (or claret) and 7-Up. If necessary add additional red wine and 7-Up, in equal quantities, along with small doses of cognac.

Sleep well...

Serves 14-16   Preparation time: 20 minutes

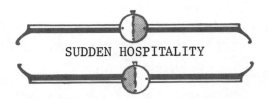

SUDDEN HOSPITALITY

1 quart orange juice
1/2 pint lemon juice, frozen, not lemonade
1 pint pineapple juice
1 quart sauterne
1 quart club soda

Pour over ice in punch bowl. Make ahead if you wish, but do not add soda until just before serving.

Serves 20   Preparation time: 20 minutes

CHERRY ICE RING

10-12 cherries

Place cherries in ring mold. Fill with water and
freeze. Run under water briefly to loosen from
mold, and place in punch bowl at serving time.

Preparation time: 5 minutes

TINGLE TEA

For easy does it...

1 package instant tea with sugar, lemon already added

Prepare according to directions. Add rum or sauterne
to taste. Serve cold.

Serves 6   Preparation time: 5 minutes

WINE SPARKLE

A delightfully refreshing drink.

1 fifth of your favorite wine
1 large bottle club soda

Mix wine with club soda in equal proportions and
serve over ice.

Serves 12   Preparation time: 5 minutes

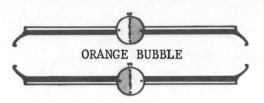

ORANGE BUBBLE

Delightful for brunches.

1 fifth champagne
1 can frozen orange juice, fixed according to directions

Combine equal parts of champagne and orange juice.
Float twig of fresh mint, if available.

Serves 8   Preparation time: 5 minutes

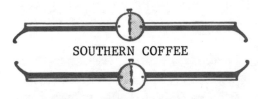

SOUTHERN COFFEE

Delightfully different after-dinner drink. Serves
as dessert when served in demi-tasse cup with cookie.

4 oz. bourbon
4 oz. cold coffee
1 cup vanilla or butter pecan ice cream
Nutmeg

Buzz in blender and sprinkle with nutmeg.

Serves 4   Preparation time: 5 minutes

HAWAIIAN HI!

1 jigger vodka
1/2 cup pineapple juice

Pour over ice and decorate with mint sprig.

Serves 1   Preparation time: 5 minutes

MOUNTAIN CLIMBER

1/2 bottle Sweet and Sour Mix
3 fifths domestic champagne
1/3 fifth brandy
1/4 small bottle lime juice
1 quart lime sherbet
2 sliced limes
1 small bottle 7-Up

Mix ingredients and serve.

Serves 14-16   Preparation time: 10 minutes

FALL FLING

Great spicy, hot fruit drink for fall, winter, and
Halloween!

1 large can apple juice
1 cinnamon stick
1 tsp. whole cloves
Muscatel or apple brandy to taste
8 lemon slices

Heat apple juice with whole cinnamon stick and whole
cloves placed in cheese cloth or tea ball. Remove
spices, pour in muscatel or apple brandy to taste
and heat just to a simmer. Serve in heavy mugs topped
with a thin slice of lemon.

Serves 8   Preparation time: 15 minutes

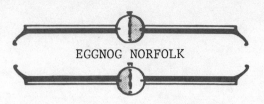

EGGNOG NORFOLK

Can be made days ahead and refrigerated.

6 eggs
3/4 cup sugar
1 pint cream
1 pint milk
1 oz. Jamaica Rum
1 pint whiskey
Grated nutmeg

Separate eggs. Add 1/2 cup sugar to egg yolks while
beating. Add 1/4 cup sugar to egg whites after beating. Add cream and milk to egg yolks. Add whiskey
and rum in slow steady stream, stirring constantly.
Lightly fold in egg whites. Chill well. Whip cream
may be used as topping, garnish with nutmeg.

Serves 10   Preparation time: 25 minutes

MORNING-AFTER PUNCH

1 quart milk
4 tbs. sugar
6 oz. light rum
2 oz. brandy
Nutmeg

Shake ingredients with 4 ice cubes or buzz in blender.
Sprinkle with nutmeg.

Serves 4   Preparation time: 10 minutes

JANUARY

FEBRUARY

MARCH

APRIL

MAY

JUNE

JULY

AUGUST

SEPTEMBER

OCTOBER

NOVEMBER

DECEMBER

Parties a GoGo

HOLIDAY TREE

This unique decorating idea is used throughout "Parties a Go Go."

Find a small pretty branch and stick it into a needle-point normally used for flower arrangements. Place in small clay pot. Spray pot with white paint. Adhere needlepoint to pot with florist's clay. Fill pot with small rocks to anchor further. Spray branch white and you're now set for any occasion...Mine has endured years of traveling around.

Your party tree can be used all year round . . . Easter eggs symbolizing rebirth...small felt hearts at Valentine's Day, fortune cookies...small Christmas balls, shamrocks on St. Pat's Day...booties and bows for baby showers....

VICTORIAN PARTY IDEA

An idea that you might borrow from the Victorian hostess who gave large parties is to have a special friend designated in each room to ensure that all guests feel especially welcome.

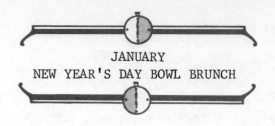

JANUARY
NEW YEAR'S DAY BOWL BRUNCH

Since practically everybody is a football fan on New
Year's Day, it's a wonderful time to get together
with a group of friends to watch the Bowl games on
television.

As for decorating: save your turkey carcass (after
making soup with it) and let it dry out. Then spray
it gold--very effective! Now fill small white bowls
with cotton balls, rose petals, sugar, oranges, etc.
to symbolize the various Bowl games.

MENU

Bloody Mary

*Sausage Stroganoff
(prepared the day ahead)

Fluffy Rice

Fruit Compote
or
*Hurry Curry Fruit

Honey   *Angel Flakes

Coffee

*Recipe included elsewhere in book. Check index for
specific pages.

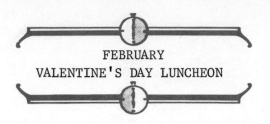

FEBRUARY
VALENTINE'S DAY LUNCHEON

Use your laciest or most delicate table cloth or
mats. Fill *Holiday Tree with red felt hearts and
carnations tucked here and there.

MENU

*Distaff Brew

*Seafeed Special   *English Pea Casserole

*Ault Aspic in Heart Shaped Mold

Peach Halves Stuffed with Cream Cheese and Mincemeat

Meringue Filled with Peppermint Ice Cream

Tea or Coffee

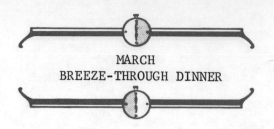

MARCH
BREEZE-THROUGH DINNER

As March is known for windy days, try quickies one
spring evening. Decorate with several of the fascinat-
ing Japanese kites or kites in any form, found easily
in import shops. Use as wall decorations, and hang
from chandelier. Cut out kite forms from colored
construction paper and attach to *Holiday Tree.

MENU

*Sangria Irlandesa

*Cannery Row Canapés

*Potato Onion Potage

*Gayle's Shrimp Brew

Fluffy Parslied Rice

*Fiesta Fruit Freeze   *Rolls Nannie

*LSD (Lemon Ice with Creme de Menthe)

Coffee or Tea

APRIL
EASTER DINNER

In almost every culture, there is a spring festival
to celebrate the reawakening of life. The egg is
the symbol of new life and the focal point in most
Easter parties. Decorate with a small Williamsburg-
type hurricane lamp filled with dyed Easter eggs.
Hang dyed Easter eggs on *Holiday Tree.

MENU

*Le Mandarin Orange

*Baked Ham ad Lib

*Noodles Afloat

*Celestial Celery

*Cinnamon Rolls Nannie

Easter Basket Dessert:
Meringue filled with 3 scoops ice cream.
Top with frozen strawberries or raspberries.

Coffee or Tea

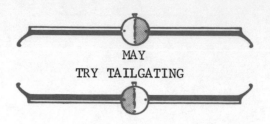

MAY

TRY TAILGATING

Let the tailgate of a station wagon provide a firm
surface for a fun family picnic. Take a small cloth
to spread on tailgate.... Upon first arriving at
your picnic location send children out to gather
bouquets of wild flowers and grasses.... Take along
several outdoor games... football, frisbee, etc....
Take also several pieces of ribbon with which to tie
the collected flowers in bunches to be displayed on
tailgate.

Your menu could be traditional and include baked beans,
potato salad, sandwiches, fresh fruit, and cup cakes...
or any GO GO recipe that happens to be a favorite of
your family.

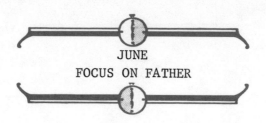

JUNE

FOCUS ON FATHER

If asked, most fathers will claim they don't need
a thing. But there's not a father in the land who
won't be tickled pink by all the tokens of affection
you can dream up for Father's Day....

You could commemorate the day with a special break-
fast, or wait till supper. Whichever you choose,
center it around his favorite sport...even if he's
only a spectator. Use symbols of his sport, or hobby,
as a centerpiece.

If he loves golf, for instance, plunge golf tees into
styrofoam covered with leaves. Secure leaves with
straight pins. Then place flower arrangement, if
desired, in center of styrofoam. Each family member
will enjoy thinking of something special to commemorate Dad's special day....

Serve Dad's favorite GO GO dishes.

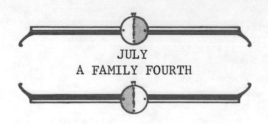

JULY
A FAMILY FOURTH

Decorate with lots of red, white, and blue balloons,
which are nice "take-homes" for the children. Lots
of little flags are fun to place around, and patriotic
red, white, and blue paperware is available.

Use sparklers or torches as evening approaches. Invite
guests to give a one-minute speech on any office they'd
like to hold... from the presidency down to local dog
catcher. Decorate soap box with crepe paper streamers.

MENU

*Children's Sparkle

*Old Crony Punch

*Wing Dings

Relish Tray

*Bev's Charcoal Burgers   Toasted Buns

*Noodle Doodle & Cheese

Watermelon   Roasted Marshmallows

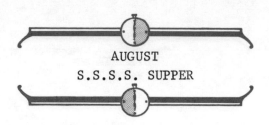

AUGUST
S.S.S.S. SUPPER

S.S.S.S. stands for Spirits, Soup, Sandwiches,
and Sweets. It's a very easy supper for summertime
entertaining. And try having your guests guess
what "S.S.S.S." stands for.

Three or four days before your S.S.S.S. supper make
Gazpacho--much better when made ahead. Two days
before, cook Roast Beef...refrigerate. The day
before, take Roast to butcher to be thinly sliced
and make Cheese Cakes Melba. On the day of the
Supper you can relax and make flower arrangements.
Set the table with felt ship signal flags hung on
*Holiday Tree. Signal flags are given in any encyclo-
pedia.

MENU

*Pisces Punch

*Wing Dings

*Gazpacho   *Roast Beef Rarity

Pickles   Rye Bread   Mustard

Pumpernickel Bread   *Roast Beef Complement

*Demi-Cheese Cakes Melba

Coffee or Tea

SEPTEMBER
SHERRY PARTY

Expecting the girls for bridge? Getting acquainted
with a new neighbor? Holding a board meeting at
your house? Chase away back-to-school blues by
inviting all the neighborhood mothers in for sherry
the first day of school.

MENU

*Sausage Biscuit Bites   *Eggs Siberia

*Cherry Tomatoes Adriatic

Pickled Okra

Marinated Green Beans

*Mystery Hors d'Oeuvre   *Oyster Dollops

Cubes of Laughing Cow Cheese Surrounded by Gingerbread
Cookies

Sherry

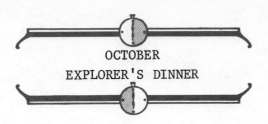

OCTOBER
EXPLORER'S DINNER

Decorate for this international theme party using styrofoam pyramids and icebergs with flags of all countries stuck in or make flower arrangement and tuck in flags.

MENU

*Mystery Hors d'Oeuvre

*Hong Kong Onion Soup

*Up-to-Date Doves   *Classic Pilaf
  or *Virginia Beach Chicken

*Mediterranean Salad   *Hurry Curry Fruit

*Brandywine Ice Cream

Coffee or Tea

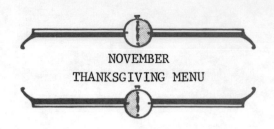

NOVEMBER
THANKSGIVING MENU

Decorate with a simple cornucopia filled with fresh
fruits and flowers and wheat. Light the house with
lots of candles to add a warm glow. For a festive
centerpiece, spray a fresh pineapple gold, leaving
top green, also spray a variety of nuts and fruits
(lemons, bananas, apples, etc.) gold. Once dry, place
on circle of styrofoam, elevating pineapple with
footed dish. Bank fruit around pineapple. Put fresh
green leaves around base (will keep about a week).

MENU

Traditional Turkey as
YOU like it...dressing...gravy

*Hot Spiced Cider

*Sausage Biscuit Bites

*Sweet Potato Harvest   *Onions Cavalier

*English Pea Casserole

*Cranberry Orange Relish   *Rolls Nannie

*Confetti Pound Cake or *Cafecoupia

Coffee or Tea

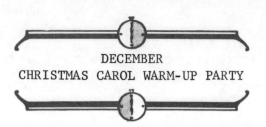

DECEMBER
CHRISTMAS CAROL WARM-UP PARTY

December is a good month to have your home smelling
of nostalgia....To create this aroma, boil 2 tbs.
whole cloves in a saucepan with a cup of water.
Light the house with candles...fire in your fireplace...
fill a Williamsburg hurricane lamp with red Christmas
balls.

MENU

Hot Chocolate
or
*Hot Spiced Cider

Christmas Cookies   *Demi-Cheese Cakes Melba

Bowl of Apples and Fruits
with Nuts

Popcorn

Note: See next page for another exciting Christmas
        idea!

CHRISTMAS TREE
BREAKFAST ROLLS

Delicious to fix the night before to munch on
Christmas morning with juice and coffee while
opening gifts. A thoughtful gift to present on
Christmas Eve to close friends.

2 9 1/2 oz. packages cinnamon refrigerated rolls
   with icing, prepared according to directions
6 tbs. chopped candied mixed fruit (red, green, etc.).

Separate rolls, arrange on a 10" by 14" greased
baking sheet in rows to simulate a Christmas Tree.
Start at the center top of baking sheet, arrange
rolls very closely in rows of 1-2-3-4-5 thru 7.
Bake in preheated oven 375 degrees for 18-20 minutes.

Remove from baking sheet onto a platter or bread
board or cut cardboad box to fit size and make a
cover out of foil. While rolls are hot, spread
with icing and sprinkle with candied fruit to
decorate.

Yields 16 individual rolls   Preparation time: 10 minute

Wine and Food Guide

These are popular choices but there are no hard and fast rules.
The right wine is the one you like the best.

Which

What

Cocktail Time

Serve chilled, without
food, or with taste
tempters, nuts, cheese

Appetizer Wines

Sherry
Vermouth
Flavored wines

Lighter Dishes

Serve well chilled, with
chicken, fish, shellfish,
omelettes, white meat

White Table Wines

Chablis
Sauterne
Rhine

Hearty Dishes

Serve at cool room
temperature with steaks,
chops, roasts, game,
cheese dishes, spaghetti

Red Table Wines

Burgundy
Chianti
Rosé

Dessert Time

Serve chilled or at cool
room temperature, with
fruit, cookies, nuts, cheese,
fruitcake, pound cake

Dessert Wines

Muscatel
Angelica
Cream sherry
Port, Tokay

All Foods

Serve well chilled with
any food—appetizers,
main course, or
desserts

Sparkling Wines

Champagne
Pink champagne
Sparkling Burgundy
Cold duck

Index

Shopper's List

Items to keep on hand for Go-Go recipes.

FOR PANTRY SHELF

Canned smoked oysters
Canned shrimp
Canned crabmeat
Cream of celery soup
Cream of mushroom soup
Cream of chicken soup
Canned red madrilene soup
Canned mushrooms
Canned macaroni and cheese sauce
Canned sweet potatoes
Spiced peaches (in jar)
Le Seur peas
Canned beef stew
Canned stewed tomatoes
Canned fruit cocktail
Canned French fried onions
Canned water chestnuts
Canned sliced peaches
Canned sliced apples
Marinated artichokes (in jar)
Marinated mushrooms (in jar)
Chipped beef (in jar)
Sweet and sour vegetable salad (in jar)
Chocolate fudge topping (in jar)
Worcestershire sauce
Italian dressing mix (in envelope)
Pimento (in jar)
Onion soup mix
Cayenne

Durkee's salad dressing
White horseradish
Mini-marshmallows
Raspberry-flavored gelatin
Wheat Thins
Ritz crackers

FOR REFRIGERATOR
Refrigerated biscuits
Sour cream
Cool Whip
Grated cheddar cheese

FOR FREEZER
Frozen pie shells
Chopped frozen onion
Chopped frozen green pepper
Unpeeled shrimp (fresh or flash frozen)
Sausage meat (bulk)
Assorted frozen vegetables
Angel food cake (store-bought)

FOR BAR
Sherry
Burgundy
Rosé
White wine